CARMEN RENE MEMORIAL SCHOOL

D1179277

ST. LUCIA
THE LAND AND THE PEOPLE

DANIEL GILPIN

WAYLAND

First published in 2010 by Wayland

Copyright © Wayland 2010

Wayland
338 Euston Road
London NW1 3BH

Wayland Australia
Level 17/207 Kent Street
Sydney NSW 2000

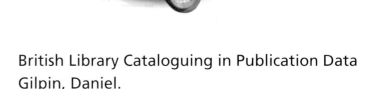

Senior editor: Debbie Foy
Designer: Stephen Prosser
Photographer: Trevor Goldsmith
Proofreader/indexer: Katie Dicker

Acknowledgements:
The author and publisher would like
to thank Carmen Rene Memorial School,
St Lucia, for their assistance with the
photographs on location.

All photography by Trevor Goldsmith except:

5, 6, 14, 44 – iStock; 14 (top), 36 – Shutterstock; 9 – Wolfgang Kaehler/CORBIS; 32 – Angelo Cavalli/GETTY; 10, 42-43 – St Lucia Tourist Board

Map illustrations by Ian Thompson

British Library Cataloguing in Publication Data
Gilpin, Daniel.
  St Lucia : the land and the people.
  1. Saint Lucia--Geography--Juvenile literature.
  2. Saint Lucia--Social conditions--Juvenile
  literature.
  3. Saint Lucia--Social life and customs--Juvenile
  literature.
  I. Title
  917.2'9843-dc22

ISBN: 978 0 7502 6319 1

Printed in China
Wayland is a division of Hachette Children's Books,
an Hachette UK company.

www.hachette.co.uk

Contents

where in the world?

St Lucia is an island between North and South America. It lies in the Caribbean Sea, on the far side of the Atlantic Ocean, more than 6,400 km from Britain.

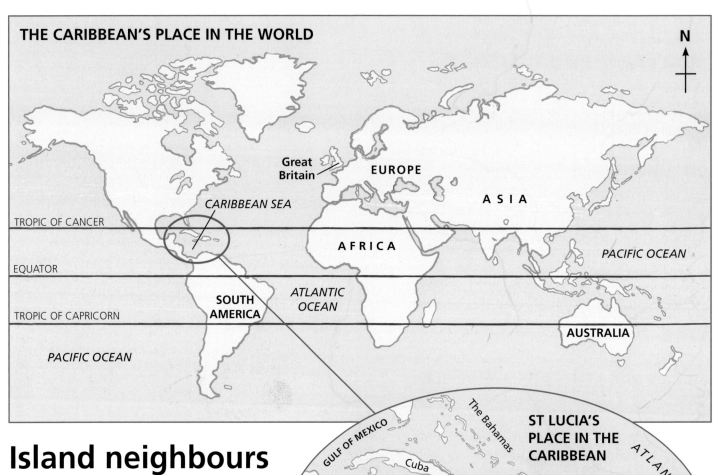

THE CARIBBEAN'S PLACE IN THE WORLD

N

Great Britain
EUROPE
ASIA
CARIBBEAN SEA
TROPIC OF CANCER
AFRICA
PACIFIC OCEAN
EQUATOR
SOUTH AMERICA
ATLANTIC OCEAN
TROPIC OF CAPRICORN
AUSTRALIA
PACIFIC OCEAN

Island neighbours

St Lucia is a small island. It sits in a group of islands known as the Windward Islands. St Lucia's nearest neighbour is the island of Martinique. Martinique lies approximately 48 km north of St Lucia. Other islands that are close to St Lucia are St Vincent, 64 km to the south, and Barbados, 174 km to the south-east.

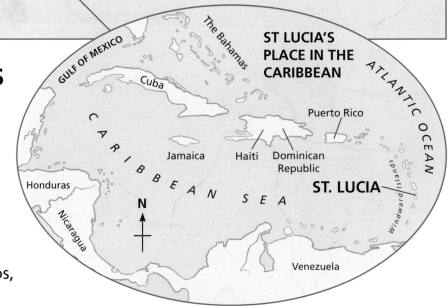

The Bahamas
ST LUCIA'S PLACE IN THE CARIBBEAN
GULF OF MEXICO
ATLANTIC OCEAN
Cuba
Puerto Rico
CARIBBEAN
Jamaica
Haiti
Dominican Republic
Honduras
ST. LUCIA
SEA
Windward Islands
N
Nicaragua
Venezuela

Feeling the heat

St Lucia is only 1,540 km north of the equator. The equator is a line found on globes and maps that runs around the middle of the Earth. Countries near the equator are hot. The farther north or south you travel from the equator, the colder it becomes. London is 5,730 km north of the equator. This explains why it is much colder there than in St Lucia.

Fast Facts

St Lucia is in the Tropics. The Tropics is the area between the Tropic of Cancer and the Tropic of Capricorn.

▲ *St Lucia is a tropical island surrounded by warm seas.*

St Lucia up close

Compared with Britain, St Lucia is a small country. Its population is also small with just 167,000 people living on the island. Britain's total population is around 61 million.

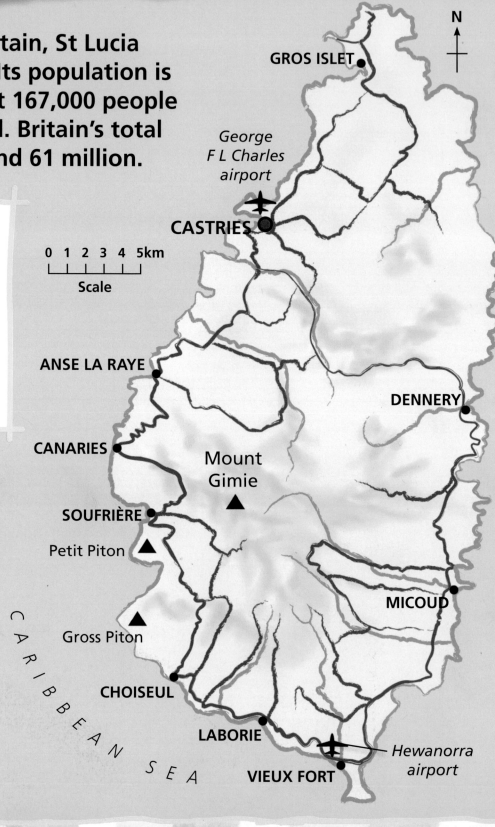

mountainous regions

▲ **mountains**

✈ **airports**

〜 roads

〜 rivers

GROS ISLET

George F L Charles airport

CASTRIES

0 1 2 3 4 5km
Scale

ANSE LA RAYE

DENNERY

CANARIES

Mount Gimie ▲

SOUFRIÈRE

Petit Piton ▲

Gross Piton ▲

MICOUD

CHOISEUL

LABORIE

Hewanorra airport

VIEUX FORT

C A R I B B E A N   S E A

VIEUX FORT

SOUFRIERE

DENNERY

CANARIES

ANSE LA RAYE

LABORIE

MICOUD

Many mountains

St Lucia is a beautiful and exciting place to live. It has high mountains, deep valleys and volcanic springs. **Inland**, there are areas of tropical rainforest, and around the coast there are rugged cliffs and spectacular sandy beaches.

The people are known as St Lucians. Most live on the coast or in large river valleys that curve inland. Much of the island of St Lucia is mountainous. Steep slopes make this inland landscape difficult to farm, so few people live there.

St Lucia stats

Length:	44 km
Width:	22 km
Area:	616 sq km
Highest point:	Mount Gimie – 958 m

Town and country

In Britain, most people live in towns or cities, but in St Lucia more than two-thirds live in the countryside. Many people work on large farms called plantations. Some also grow food for themselves, near to their own homes.

Focus on...

St Lucia's flag

▼ *St Lucia's flag was designed by the artist Dunstan St Omer, who was born in Castries in 1927.*

In 1979, St Lucia became independent from Britain and so a new national flag was created. Each of the flag's colours is significant. The black and white represent the black and white communities that live in harmony on the island. The yellow triangle stands for St Lucia's golden beaches, and the blue stands for the sea. The two triangles formed by the white and black of the flag represent the Pitons – St Lucia's most famous landmark.

Weather and climate

Like most places in the tropics, St Lucia is hot most of the year, but also wet. Each month, on average, St Lucia has more than twice as much rain as London. Some months it has four times as much!

▼ *Daytimes are usually dry. Warm, night-time rain helps to produce lush, green plants.*

Downpour!

Drizzly rain is very rare in St Lucia. Instead, rain comes in very heavy downpours. Fortunately for St Lucians and visiting tourists, it often rains at night. By mid-morning, the clouds have usually disappeared and the sun comes out.

► *This graph shows the rainfall and temperature patterns in St Lucia.*

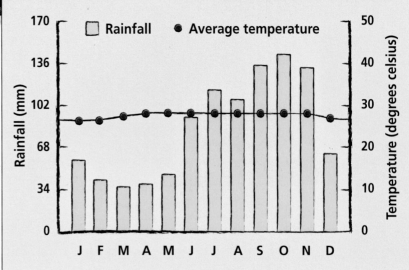

Hurricanes

St Lucia often has tropical storms during the wet season. Occasionally, these can be very powerful. The most devastating storms are called hurricanes. When hurricanes strike, they can cause a great deal of damage. Their winds may blow down trees and rip the roofs from buildings. On average, hurricanes only strike St Lucia about once every four years. For the islanders, they have become part of life. After a hurricane has passed, the damage is repaired and life goes on as before.

Although hurricanes are rare, it rains in St Lucia nearly every day.

Hot and humid

Winter temperatures in St Lucia are similar to the highest summer temperatures we have in Britain. But, unlike Britain, temperatures in St Lucia stay fairly constant throughout the year. On average, it is only two or three degrees hotter in the summer than it is in winter.

Rainfall in St Lucia varies a lot over the year. The driest months are January to May (although even then there is much more rain in St Lucia than in Britain). From June until December, rainfall more than doubles. These months make up St Lucia's wet season.

A volcanic land

The island of St Lucia is formed from several ancient volcanoes. These erupted on the sea floor and poured out lava, which quickly cooled and turned into solid rock.

As more lava erupted and cooled, the volcanoes grew and rose up above the sea's surface. Over millions of years, the lava eruptions started to join together. By about 3 million years ago, they formed the shape of St Lucia as it is today.

▲ *The Pitons are volcanic plugs – solid lava that once filled ancient volcanoes.*

Bubbling springs

St Lucia has not seen a major volcanic eruption for about 40,000 years, but there is still a lot of hot rock beneath the surface. The heat from these rocks is passed into water deep under the ground, and the water emerges as hot, bubbling springs.

The most famous hot springs in St Lucia are in a volcanic crater near the town of Soufrière. The Sulphur Springs are a popular tourist attraction. People come to see the hot steam (which smells of rotten eggs) and the bubbling, muddy pools.

▶ *Steam rises from the ground at Sulphur Springs in the south-west of the island.*

Earthquake risks

St Lucia often has small earthquakes, especially around Soufrière and Sulphur Springs, but larger earthquakes sometimes affect the whole island. In 2007, St Lucia was hit by a major earthquake. Nobody was hurt, but many buildings were damaged.

Into the Future: Natural energy

In volcanic areas like St Lucia, the rocks underground are extremely hot. This heat can be used to make electricity. Water is pumped down into the rocks and boils underground, creating steam. This steam is then used to drive machines called turbines, which turn generators, to make electricity.

Scientists call the heat that is generated from underground rocks geothermal energy. At the moment, St Lucia does not have any geothermal power stations, but it could do in the future. It would then be able to stop **importing** expensive oil for its power stations, as it does today.

In the wild

Long ago, the island of St Lucia was covered in lush rainforest. Today, much of it has been chopped down, but in the hills and mountains some rainforest remains untouched and is a rich habitat for exotic wildlife.

▶ *St Lucia has dozens of small rivers. As they flow down from high ground, many plunge over waterfalls like this one.*

▲ *Exotic flowers such as this Heliconia grow throughout St Lucia.*

Unique wildlife

Some wildlife can only be found in St Lucia. The most famous of these unique creatures is the St Lucia parrot, also known as the jacquot. Once hunted, the jacquot is now protected and is becoming more common in the forests. It is St Lucia's national bird.

The jacquot shares the rainforests with other creatures, such as snakes and lizards. The largest snake is the St Lucia boa which can grow to more than 4 m long!

▶ *The jacquot feeds on rainforest fruit. Although its numbers are growing, it is still rare. Around 500 jacquots live in the wild.*

Into the Future: Saved from the chainsaw!

Over the years, many of St Lucia's rainforests have been cut down to make way for buildings, roads and farmland. This process is known as **deforestation**. However, the rainforests that are left in St Lucia are now protected. In these areas, it is against the law to hunt wildlife or cut down trees. The animals and plants that live in these special places are now left in peace.

The night shift

Snakes and lizards are often seen in the rainforests because they are active during the day. **Nocturnal** creatures only come out at night. St Lucia's most common nocturnal **mammals** are bats.

Bats feed on insects or fruit, but the greater bulldog bat catches fish by hooking them with its long claws, which it drags through the water while flying over the surface.

◀ *This man is holding a St Lucia boa. Boas are not poisonous, but kill their prey by squeezing the animal until it cannot breathe.*

The sea and its shore

St Lucia is famous for its sandy beaches, and tourists from all over the world spend holidays there. Its coast also has cliffs, mangrove forests and coral reefs rich with wildlife. The coast is where most St Lucians live.

▼ *Most reef fish are very colourful, like this angel fish.*

St Lucia's coral reefs are home to all sorts of animals.

Homes by the water

St Lucia is a mountainous island and few people live inland. Instead, they cluster around the coast in villages, towns and cities. Here, the land is flatter and easier to farm, and there is access to the sea. Seafood has long been important to St Lucians, making up a large part of what many people eat.

◀ *Many St Lucian towns have buildings that crowd right down to the beach. As this picture shows, trees often grow between the houses.*

Crashing waves

St Lucia's coastline has been shaped by the sea. Most of the island's cliffs are on the east coast, facing the Atlantic Ocean, where huge waves crash against the shore, especially during stormy weather.

The west coast is quieter and where most of the island's sandy beaches are found. More people live on the west coast than the east coast, partly because the seas are calmer and it is much safer for boats to leave the shore.

FOCUS On...

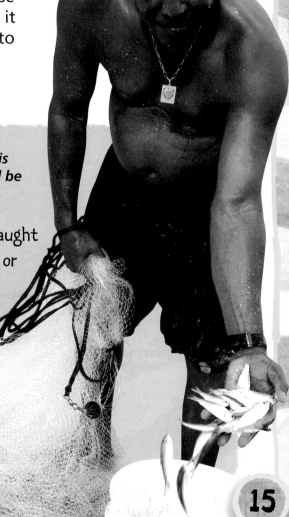

▶ *The small fish this man has caught will be sold in the market.*

Fishing

Many St Lucian men make their living from fishing. Fish are caught in the traditional way using nets that are pulled into a circle or dragged through the water. Some fishermen catch lobsters and fish from the seabed using traps. The island has around 2,500 fishermen, working full-time and part-time. The busiest fishing months are from December to June. During this time, large fish such as wahoo and tuna become more common as they move closer to shore.

St Lucia's towns and cities are small compared to those in Britain. The island has one city (Castries, the capital) and three main towns: Soufrière, Gros Islet and Vieux Fort. There are also many villages.

Castries is the largest **urban** area on the island. Although it is St Lucia's capital city, it is actually smaller than many British towns. Most St Lucian people live in the countryside, whereas in Britain 90 per cent of people live in towns or cities.

Spacious streets

Even St Lucia's built-up areas are more spacious than most towns in Britain. People often live in single-storey detached houses. Semi-detached homes and terraced houses are rare on the island. Outside Castries, roads are wide though there is little traffic. Most town gardens are very lush with large, leafy plants.

▲ *Most buildings in St Lucia are just one storey high. Many, such as this restaurant, are painted with bright colours.*

A wealthy port

Many of St Lucia's towns started as small fishing villages. Castries was first settled in the 1760s, when the island was a French **colony**. Castries Bay provided a safe harbour for French ships and the city remains the island's most important port today.

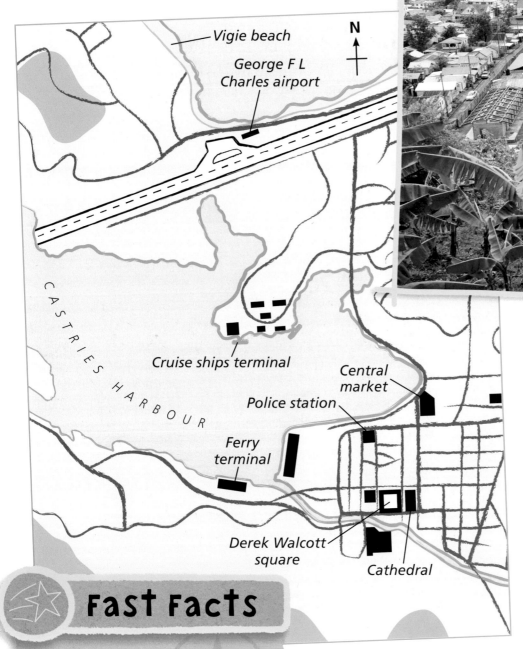

▲ *This is the town of Soufrière, on the island's west coast. Soufrière is an important town, but it is much smaller than Castries.*

Castries developed quickly due to the profits it made from **trading**. Sugar and other **goods** left the island from Castries, and supplies from overseas were imported. Wealthy merchants built their homes there and even though it has poorer neighbourhoods, Castries is still the home of many of the island's richest people.

Map labels:
- Vigie beach
- N
- George F L Charles airport
- CASTRIES HARBOUR
- Cruise ships terminal
- Central market
- Police station
- Ferry terminal
- Derek Walcott square
- Cathedral

Fast Facts

Castries was named after an important French official, the Marquis de Castries, in 1785.

▲ *This map of Castries shows how the city is built around its harbour. North of the capital is the George F L Charles airport.*

Life on the land

Over half of St Lucians live in the countryside and one-fifth work in agriculture. In Britain, less than 1.5 per cent of the population work in agriculture.

Most St Lucian farmers grow plants of one type or another. The tropical climate and rich volcanic soils are perfect for this type of farming. Farmers grow a range of fruit and vegetables, but the most common crop is bananas, which are grown on plantations. Once harvested, the bananas are taken to Castries and loaded onto ships for **export**.

Into the Future: Organic farming

Organic farming avoids using **pesticides** or other artificial chemicals, and is becoming more popular on the island. Farmers find that they can sell organic food for higher prices than non-organic food. St Lucia's hotels, in particular, buy organic foods that have been grown locally.

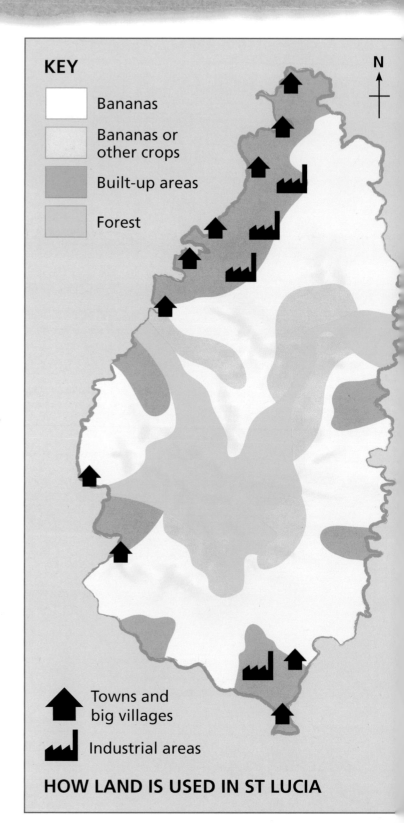

KEY

- Bananas
- Bananas or other crops
- Built-up areas
- Forest

- Towns and big villages
- Industrial areas

HOW LAND IS USED IN ST LUCIA

Local produce

Growing food for export is important, but St Lucia also produces much of its own food, too. St Lucia's farms produce enough tomatoes, onions, carrots, cabbages and **breadfruit** to feed everyone who lives on or visits the island.

▶ *Most St Lucians walk to their local market to buy fresh fruit and vegetables.*

FOCUS On...

A Day in the Life... of a banana plantation worker

Sometimes, he helps by washing picked bananas and packing them into crates. On other days, he drives the delivery truck that takes the bananas to Castries, where they are loaded onto ships.

James works on a banana plantation. He decides which fruit should be cut down and directs the planting and **cultivation** of new banana trees.

"We get a fair price from the UK supermarkets, but it costs us a lot to maintain a plantation like this. We have thousands of trees!"

Island homes

Most St Lucians live in houses. There are hardly any flats on the island – apart from those used by tourists. Houses come in all sorts of shapes and sizes, just as they do in Britain.

Nearly all of St Lucia's houses are detached and there is often space or garden areas between the homes. Even the smallest houses on the island have a little land around them.

▲ *Like many St Lucian buildings, this house is made of wood.*

Many houses in the countryside are quite old, and some have been standing for centuries. New buildings are found in the towns. In Castries, nearly all buildings are less than 70 years old, since a fire in 1948 destroyed most of the city, and many homes had to be rebuilt.

◀ *In hilly areas, most houses are built on stilts.*

Bungalows on stilts

Many St Lucian houses have a similar style. Smaller houses often have one storey and may be raised up off the ground. The front door is reached by climbing a flight of steps. It is common to build raised houses in the Caribbean because stilts make it easier to build on sloping ground.

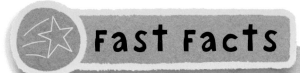

▲ *This house is built on stilts and is made of concrete instead of wood.*

The bigger houses in St Lucia are mostly owned by farmers and plantation owners. Others have been turned into hostels or hotels for tourists. Some new, large homes have been built – often for wealthy people who have moved to St Lucia to retire.

▲ *Inside a typical St Lucian house. The floors are tiled and large windows make it bright and airy.*

family life

St Lucian families are often large, with four or more children. In some families, the mother and father live together with their children. In others, the mother raises her children alone, while the father lives elsewhere.

► *A typical St Lucian family outside their home.*

▲ *When it is wet outside, children play indoors. These children are playing dominoes.*

Busy households

Many St Lucians share their homes with other relatives. This is known as an extended family. St Lucians are brought up to feel responsible towards their families, and many look after their own elderly parents.

Most children help out around the home and in other ways. In the countryside, children sometimes help out on their parents' farms, or do domestic jobs such as fetching water. In **rural** areas, many people still fetch their water from wells or standpipes in the street.

Relatives abroad

Nowadays, many islanders have relatives overseas. In the 1950s many St Lucians moved to Britain. Some **emigrants** send money back home to their families in St Lucia.

Not everyone who left the island moved far away. Some emigrants simply moved to the other Caribbean islands. These people try to keep in touch with their families back in St Lucia and still think of the island as their real home.

▶ *Weddings are important family events in St Lucia, just as they are in Britain.*

Focus on...

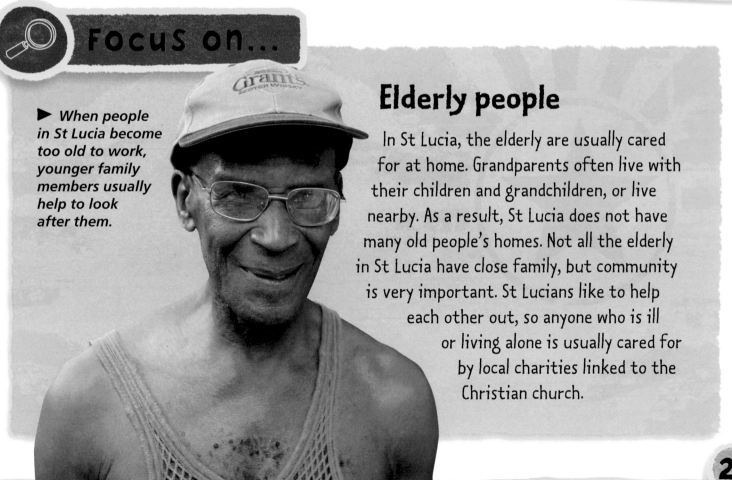

▶ *When people in St Lucia become too old to work, younger family members usually help to look after them.*

Elderly people

In St Lucia, the elderly are usually cared for at home. Grandparents often live with their children and grandchildren, or live nearby. As a result, St Lucia does not have many old people's homes. Not all the elderly in St Lucia have close family, but community is very important. St Lucians like to help each other out, so anyone who is ill or living alone is usually cared for by local charities linked to the Christian church.

Fresh food to eat

Many of the islanders' ancestors came from other parts of the world, such as West Africa. Most St Lucian dishes come from France, Africa or other Caribbean islands.

grated carrot

tomatoes

green fig and salt fish salad

plantains

cucumber salad

▶ *This is a typical St Lucian light lunch.*

Local produce

St Lucians often cook with home-grown ingredients or foods that can be bought in local markets. Plantains, coconuts, fish and seafood are popular local foods. Plaintains look like bananas, but are larger and not as sweet.

young breadfruit

plantains

Not all St Lucians have African or European ancestors. The town of Vieux Fort has an established Indian community, who started arriving on the island in the nineteenth century. They cook roti, dahl and other Indian dishes, as well as traditional St Lucian food.

◀ *This man is preparing a fresh, young coconut so that he can drink coconut milk.*

Focus on...

Home-grown food

Many St Lucians grow fruit and vegetables in home gardens, to use in their cooking. Soils are so rich that crops do not need much land to produce plenty of food. Popular home-grown fruit and vegetables include taro, watermelons, mangoes, peppers and tomatoes. Some people grow so much food that they have some left over to sell. After harvesting, they take it to the local market to make a bit of extra money.

▶ *Many people sell fruit and vegetables to make extra money. This lady has her own roadside stall.*

Cook the St Lucian way!

Why not try making this delicious avocado side dish to serve with salted cod, fishcakes or curried rice?

You will need:

- 500 g avocados (with stones)
- 125 g cassava meal (also called gari)
- Juice of half a lime
- Salt and pepper, to taste
- Avocado slices, to garnish

Makes 12 avocado balls

2 With the help of an adult, carefully cut the avocados in half and remove the stones.

1 Peel the avocados.

3 Mash the avocados with a fork until soft, then add the lime juice.

4 Add the cassava meal and knead. Season with salt and pepper to taste and knead the mixture until all the ingredients are combined.

5 Roll the mixture into balls.

6 Garnish with avocado slices. Serve and enjoy!

Shopping on the island

Most people in Britain shop at supermarkets. St Lucians often go to open-air markets to buy food, particularly local vegetables, fruit and other produce.

Market produce is fresher and cheaper than food sold in supermarkets. Castries' central market is the largest on the island, selling food, clothes and other goods. Most people head to the market in the morning – before the sun comes up and it gets too hot!

▲ *Most villages have small shops like this one, selling sweets and other food.*

Money matters

Most St Lucians earn less than British people. The average **annual income** is £4,120, compared to £23,500 in Britain. St Lucians have enough money to live on and can save money by growing food, but few earn enough to pay for luxuries. Instead, they normally only buy the goods they really need. Shopping for fun is left to the wealthiest islanders and tourists.

▼ *Castries' central market is open every day of the week except Sunday. The large parasols offer customers shade from the hot sun.*

In Britain, people often have money left over after shopping for food. Some children are given pocket money and their parents spend money on cars or things for the home. In Britain, we take these kinds of luxuries for granted.

Most St Lucian people have a different attitude when it comes to money. They have less to spend, but this does not stop them enjoying life. In St Lucia, many people make things for their homes, or toys for their children, rather than going out and buying them.

Fast Facts

One in five households on the island of St Lucia does not have a television.

▲ *St Lucian children enjoy a simple, outdoor lifestyle. These children are skipping in a playground after school.*

Religion and church

Christianity was brought to the island by the French in the seventeenth century. Today, most people in St Lucia are Roman Catholic. Some of the island's churches date back to the time of French rule, but others are more modern.

▲ *People wear their best clothes to go to church.*

▲ *This is St Joseph's Church in the town of Gros Islet.*

Religion is very important to St Lucian people. The majority of people go to church on Sunday, dressed in their finest clothes. As well as Roman Catholic churches, there are other Christian churches, too, such as Anglican, Baptist, Methodist, Pentecostal and Seventh Day Adventist.

Christianity in daily life

St Lucians celebrate many Christian festivals. Christian charities also help the poorest and most disadvantaged people on the island.

Many schools are funded by the Catholic Church, and St Lucian children attend Sunday School and are brought up to believe in God. At home, children say prayers before bedtime and families usually say Grace (a special prayer to thank God for food) before each meal.

▲ *Music is an important part of Christian worship on the island.*

Other beliefs

Not all St Lucians are Christian. The island's Indian community are Hindus or Muslims. Hindus worship many gods. Muslims follow Islam and a holy book called the Koran. St Lucia also has **atheists**, although atheism is less common in St Lucia than it is in Britain.

▲ *Like most churches in St Lucia, St Joseph's church is very clean and well looked after.*

Fast Facts

Some Christian islanders believe in a traditional folk religion from West Africa called Obeah. In this religion, herbal potions are used to keep away evil spirits and heal the sick.

Festival time!

Festivals in St Lucia are a time for fun! As most people are Catholic, the islanders celebrate many religious events. Some of these celebrations are familiar to us in Britain.

St Lucians celebrate Christmas with cards and presents. They also eat special food, including Caribbean Christmas cake made with fruit, rum, sugar and spices. The religious side of Christmas is more important to many St Lucians than it is to most Britons. Most people go to midnight mass on Christmas Eve and every year, choirs come together to sing in a special carol festival.

► *St Lucian's love colour, and carnival is the most colourful time of all.*

Further celebrations

Other reasons to celebrate include Easter, and All Saints' Day on 1st November. One of the most important non-religious festivals is National Day, held on 13th December. This is a holiday for everyone, and celebrates the day that the island became an independent country. Sports and cultural events are held, and towns and villages on the island are decorated with lanterns.

▲ *Carnival is all about dressing up and having a good time. Children and adults dance together and parade in the streets.*

FOCUS ON...

Carnival

Carnival is the biggest celebration of the year and a time for relaxation and enjoyment. It used to be held around Shrove Tuesday (Mardi Gras) as in other Catholic countries. Nowadays, it is held in July to encourage tourists to come to St Lucia.

During carnival, people dress up in fancy costumes to dance and parade through the streets, on foot or on decorated trucks. **Steel bands** and other musicians play. Carnival takes place in three of St Lucia's towns: Castries, Vieux Fort and Soufrière.

▲ *Some carnival costumes are really spectacular. This one has been made to look like a giant mask.*

School and play

All St Lucian children go to primary school between the ages of 5 and 11. They learn many subjects, including mathematics and English. Lessons are taught in English, even though many of the children speak Creole at home.

CARMEN RENE MEMORIAL SCHOOL

Secondary school

At the age of 11, some children go to secondary school, but first they must pass a test. There is a lot of competition for places in secondary schools. Children have to study hard, and some families even pay for extra lessons to help their children pass the test.

▲ *In most primary schools in St Lucia, children wear uniforms, just as they do in Britain.*

Staying at primary school

Children who do not pass the test for secondary school either stay at their primary school for a few more years, or go to one of St Lucia's two senior primary schools. These only take children from the age of 11, and teach more basic subjects.

▶ *Children know school is important and try to study hard.*

Out of school fun!

Outside school hours and at weekends, children spend a lot of time playing. Some enjoy sports such as football and cricket, and some children join organised teams as they get older.

St Lucian children spend far less time playing computer games than British children. Although many homes have televisions, there are few computers or games consoles because they are too expensive for many families.

FoCuS on...

A Day in the Life... of a St Lucian schoolgirl

Jenelle Gilda Lewis is 10 years old. She was born in Boston, USA, but now lives in St Lucia with her grandmother.

Jenelle attends Carmen Rene Memorial School, a primary school in Sans Souci, near Castries. Although school does not start until 9.00 am, she wakes up at 5.30 am. After eating breakfast, she walks to her cousin's house for a lift into school. School finishes at 3.00 pm. When she leaves school, Jenelle would like to be a singer, doctor, actress, movie producer or author.

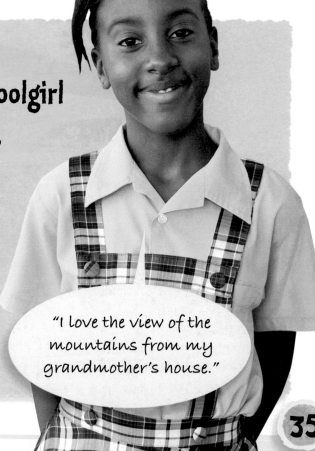

"I love the view of the mountains from my grandmother's house."

Getting around

St Lucia is a small country, so nobody ever has to travel very far. Many people hardly travel at all, but instead spend most of their lives within walking distance of home.

Compared with Britain, few St Lucians own a car. Most people use **public transport** for longer journeys. St Lucia does not have a rail system and buses that people travel on are much smaller than those in Britain.

St Lucia's minibuses are privately owned, as taxis are in Britain. The main bus station is in Castries, and minibuses travel from it to all parts of the island. There are bus stops to wait at, but people can get on or off a bus wherever they like.

▲ *Water taxis are a popular way of getting around in St Lucia.*

▲ *This minibus stop has a roof for shelter when it rains.*

Travelling abroad

Many St Lucians have relatives who live abroad. These countries could be neighbouring islands or they could be distant countries across the sea.

Ferries sail from St Lucia to other Caribbean islands. There are also two airports on the island. Flights to other Caribbean islands fly from George FL Charles airport. Flights to other destinations fly from Hewanorra International airport near Vieux Fort.

▲ *This minibus is for private hire.*

Into the Future: Public transport

Public transport is better for the environment than private vehicles. Buses and trains carry more people, and so use less fuel than when people drive their own cars.

Travelling by public transport is also cheaper. As well as buying the car, there is road tax, repairs and fuel to pay for. Most St Lucians use buses for long journeys and make shorter journeys on foot. Few people own cars, so they are not tempted to use them for short journeys, as people in Britain often do.

Making a living

Most St Lucians work for a living, but not everyone who is old enough to work has a job. The unemployment rate on the island is 20 per cent, compared with 8 per cent in Britain.

▲ *Around 1,000 people work in the St Lucian police force.*

▲ *This man is working in the fields cutting sugar cane.*

Traditionally, most St Lucians worked in agriculture, but recently things have started to change. The island now has more competition from other countries, and bananas (its main crop) do not sell as well abroad as they once did. Because of this, plantation owners cannot afford to employ as many people as they used to do.

This teacher enjoys her job at Carmen Rene Memorial School, Castries.

A Day in the Life... of a city worker

David Olanitekun works for a busy high street bank in Castries.

Like many people, David works from Monday to Friday. He gets up at 6:30 am and takes the bus to start work in the central district of Castries. David works behind the main counter, helping customers deposit and withdraw money from their bank accounts. He works as part of a team and enjoys his job.

New jobs

As agriculture has dwindled, people have had to find different kinds of work. Today, more people work in factories than on farms or plantations. Some factories make electrical parts, which are exported abroad to make electronic household goods.

Many St Lucians now work in service industries, such as banking and tourism. Since Independence, more tourists have been coming to St Lucia, and today a large part of the country's population works in its resorts and hotels.

Fast Facts

In St Lucia, 41 per cent of all paid jobs are performed by women.

"I like helping people to manage their money and I always try to have a smile for my customers."

Trade with other countries

St Lucia produces most of its own food, but some products, such as breakfast cereals and tinned goods, are imported from other countries. Imported products arrive at Castries on container ships and some are brought in by air.

St Lucia does not have the resources to make everything that it needs. Items such as televisions, computers and cars are imported from abroad. Many clothes are imported, too.

▲ Castries port is crowded with containers that have been offloaded from ships.

▶ All electrical goods in St Lucia are imported from other countries.

Import and export

St Lucia also exports many goods, bringing extra money into the country. The island's main export is still bananas, although demand is reducing. St Lucia's bananas are sold in supermarkets and shops across Britain and are known as Windward Islands bananas.

The bananas are exported on special container ships. They leave St Lucia green and unripe, but ripen up on the voyage.

▶ *Geest Line is the main shipping company to transport cargo between St Lucia and Britain.*

St Lucia's other main exports include clothes and electrical components. Other products made in St Lucia for export overseas include corrugated cardboard boxes and chocolate!

Fairtrade

Fairtrade ensures farmers get a fair price for the food they produce. In the past, St Lucian farmers were paid very little. People bought their goods for a low price, then sold them to somebody else for a lot more. These 'middle men' made lots of money, while the farmers had barely enough to live on.

Fairtrade cuts out the 'middle men' by selling direct to supermarkets in countries such as Britain. This means that the farmers get a fair price for the food they produce – enough to live on and to pay their workers.

▼ *Most of the Fairtrade bananas we buy in Britain come from St Lucia.*

Visiting St Lucia

Every year, around 300,000 people visit St Lucia. Some may be day-trippers who are on a cruise of the Caribbean. Others stay for longer, enjoying everything the island has to offer on a honeymoon or family holiday.

▶ St Lucia is many people's idea of a tropical paradise.

▲ Warm seas and sandy beaches make the island popular with families.

Money from overseas

Tourists who come to St Lucia are very important to the island's economy. The money they spend in the island's hotels, resorts and shops has helped to make St Lucia a much wealthier country than it used to be. It has also helped to create many new jobs for St Lucian people in both the towns and countryside areas.

► *Luxury cruise ships can often be seen docked in Castries harbour.*

Arriving on the island

Most British visitors to St Lucia either arrive by cruise ship or by aeroplane. Cruise ships dock in Castries harbour. International flights land at Hewanorra International airport near Vieux Fort.

"It's nice to see the smiles of people I advise about unfamiliar places. I can truly make a difference to people's holidays."

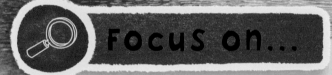

FOCUS ON...

A Day in the Life... of a tour organiser

Sharna

Sharna Benjamin works for a holiday company and organises tours around St Lucia.

Sharna normally works alone, visiting tourists at hotels around the island. Her day starts at 6.00 am when she gets up and has breakfast. She starts work two hours later, usually finishing by 5.00 pm. Sharna enjoys her job and finds it very rewarding!

43

How has St Lucia changed?

Millions of years ago, St Lucia was covered in rainforest and home only to wildlife. The first people – the Arawaks – arrived about 2,200 years ago from South America. The Arawaks were later replaced by another group of settlers, called the Caribs.

European influence

The arrival of the Arawaks and Caribs did not really affect St Lucia. The real change came when the Europeans arrived. The first settlers were Dutch soldiers, who built a base at Vieux Fort in around 1600. French and British settlers soon followed. The first sugar plantations were French, and French influence continues today in the island's **Creole** language.

▲ *Old slave huts such as these can still be seen in some parts of the island.*

The Europeans brought slaves from Africa to work on the plantations. When slavery was abolished in 1834, most of the island's people were of African origin. Their descendants still make up the majority of St Lucia's population today.

Independence

St Lucia used to be part of the British Empire, a group of countries governed by the United Kingdom. In 1979, St Lucia became an independent nation, with its own government and laws. The St Lucian parliament has a prime minister, who is voted into power by the public. Elections take place every five years. Although it is now independent, St Lucia still has the British monarch as its head of state, and whose portrait remains on its coins and bank notes.

▲ **For a long time Britain and France fought to rule St Lucia. This cannon dates back to those days.**

Recent changes and the future

The large sugar plantations on St Lucia have now been replaced by farms and plantations growing other crops. Most other big changes have been due to the growth of the island's tourist industry. As well as new hotels and shops, several modern roads have been built.

The St Lucian government hopes that the island will develop further. This depends on two main things: maintaining high levels of banana export and attracting even more tourists to the island.

▲ **St Lucian people are hopeful for the future.**

ART AND DESIGN

- Draw or paint a picture of the famous St Lucia parrot.
- Design a new logo for the St Lucia Tourist Board. Think about what St Lucia has to offer tourists and try to include those things in your design.

GEOGRAPHY

- Think about how St Lucia is different from where you live. Make a list of the differences and see how many you can come up with.

DESIGN AND TECHNOLOGY

- Design a really useful hat that people could wear in St Lucia. Think about the weather on the island when coming up with your design, and what would be the best materials to use.

MUSIC

- Choir singing is popular in St Lucia. Try singing a traditional Caribbean song as a choir with your class.

PHYSICAL EDUCATION

- Cricket is a popular sport in St Lucia. Learn the rules of cricket and organise a game!

ENGLISH

- Imagine you are on holiday in St Lucia. Write a postcard home.
- Imagine you have a pen pal in St Lucia. Write a letter telling them all about where you live.

Things to make and do

SCIENCE

- It rains much more in St Lucia than most people think. Make a rain gauge to find out how much rain falls in a week near your home.

HISTORY

- Slavery was abolished in St Lucia in 1834, a year after it had been abolished in Britain. Using the Internet or books from the library, find out when slavery was abolished in France and in the United States.
- In 1979, St Lucia achieved Independence. Using the Internet, type "Britain 1979" into Google (www.google.co.uk) to discover what was happening here in that year.

MATHS

- St Lucia is 1,540 km north of the equator. London is 5,730 km north of the equator. How much farther north of the equator is London than St Lucia?

ICT

- St Lucia is part of the Commonwealth. Use a computer at school or at home to visit http://www.thecommonwealth.org and find out more about this group of countries.

RELIGIOUS EDUCATION

- Most St Lucians are Roman Catholics. Use library books or the Internet to find out more about the Roman Catholic Church.

46

Glossary

Agriculture
Another word for farming.

Annual income
The amount of money earned by a person in a year.

Atheist
A person who does not believe in God.

Breadfruit
A melon-sized fruit with starchy flesh that, when cooked, tastes a little like freshly baked bread.

Colony
A group of people who come to settle in a new country.

Creole
A slightly altered version of the French language, spoken in St Lucia.

Cultivation
To grow or produce crops.

Deforestation
The large-scale removal of forests to make way for buildings or farming.

Emigrants
People who leave their own country to settle in another.

Eruption
A volcanic explosion, usually with lots of smoke and lava.

Export
To send goods usually by air or sea to another country.

Goods
Food or man-made objects that are made to be sold.

Habitat
A place or area where a particular type of living thing is normally found.

Importing
To bring goods in from another country.

Inland
An area away from the coast.

Lava
Liquid rock. Lava is extremely hot and sets fire to anything it touches.

Mangrove
A tropical tree with roots that grow above ground.

Mammal
An animal that feeds its young on milk. Most mammals have fur or hair. We are mammals, and so are cats and dogs.

Nocturnal
Creatures that are active at night and sleep or rest during the day.

Pesticides
Chemicals used to kill insects or other pests.

Public transport
Vehicles that anyone can ride in, by buying a ticket or paying a fare.

Rural
To do with the countryside.

Steel band
A band that plays steel drums, a traditional Caribbean instrument.

Trading
Buying things from or selling things to other people.

Unemployment rate
The number of people of working age who do not have a job.

Urban
To do with towns or cities.

Books, websites and index

Books to read:

The Landscape of St Lucia, Alison Brownlie Bojang (Wayland, 2001)

The People of St Lucia, Alison Brownlie Bojang (Wayland, 2001)

Living in St Lucia Pupils' Book, Vincent Bunce and Wendy Morgan (Cambridge University Press, 1996)

Living in St Lucia Teacher's Book, Vincent Bunce and Wendy Morgan (Cambridge University Press, 1996)

Useful websites:

http://www.stlucia.org
This is the official website of the St Lucia Tourist Board and offers an interactive map of the island.

http://www.geographia.com/st-lucia
This website offers lots of information on the island's tourist attractions.

http://www.lonelyplanet.com/st-lucia
This website has lots of facts about St Lucia and is a great travel guide to the island.

Index